Walking the Road to Freedom

Walking the Road to Freedom

A Story about Sojourner Truth

by Jeri Ferris

illustrations by Peter E. Hanson

A Carolrhoda Creative Minds Book

Carolrhoda Books, Inc./Minneapolis

For Tom

This book is available in two editions:
Library binding by Carolrhoda Books, Inc.,
a division of Lerner Publishing Group
Soft cover by First Avenue Editions,
an imprint of Lerner Publishing Group
241 First Avenue North
Minneapolis, MN 55401 U.S.A.

Website address: www.lernerbooks.com

Library of Congress Cataloging-in-Publication Data

Ferris, Jeri.
   Walking the road to freedom.
(A Carolrhoda creative minds book)
   Summary: Traces the life of the Black woman orator who spoke out against
slavery throughout New England and the Midwest.
   1. Truth, Sojourner, d. 1883—Juvenile literature. 2. Afro-Americans—
Biography—Juvenile literature. 3. Abolitionists—United States—
Biography—Juvenile literature. [Truth, Sojourner, d. 1883. 2. Afro-
Americans—biography. 3. Abolitionists. 4. Reformers] I. Hanson,
Peter E., ill. II. Title. III. Series.
E185.97.T8F47 1988   305.5'67'0924[B][92]   87-18277
ISBN 0-87614-318-4 (lib. bdg. : alk. paper)
ISBN 0-87614-505-5 (pbk. : alk. paper)

Manufactured in the United States of America
   19 20 21 22 23 – MA – 06 05 04 03 02 01

Table of Contents

AUTHOR'S NOTE

Sojourner Truth was born into slavery in New York in about 1797 or 1798. She never knew for sure which year she was born or even whether it was summer or winter. Her owner probably wrote it down, just as he wrote down when the calves and pigs and sheep were born, but his records are lost.

When Sojourner was born, her name wasn't Sojourner Truth. It was Isabelle Hardenbergh. Her mother named her Isabelle, but slaves didn't have their own last names, only their owner's name. Since Isabelle's master was Charles Hardenbergh, Hardenbergh became her last name. And since every time a slave was sold to a different owner the slave took the new owner's name, Isabelle had several different last names before she finally became Sojourner Truth.

Although there were many slaves in northern New York, where Isabelle was born, slave owning was not a way of life in the northern states as it was in the southern states. On the large southern cotton plantations, slaves worked year-round, from dawn to dark, trying to stay ahead of the overseer's whip. In the North the farms were smaller, and no farming could be done at all during the long, cold winters. Slavery wasn't very practical in the North, and what's more, many people believed it wasn't right.

In 1785 New York passed a law forbidding any new slaves to be sold into the state and forbidding the sale of any New York slaves out of the state. In 1799 another new law freed any slave girl born after July 4, 1799, when she became 25 years old.

Unfortunately for Isabelle, she was born *before* July 4, 1799. But Isabelle became Sojourner Truth, and she did something about slavery.

Chapter One

"Sold! For $50, the Negro girl Isabelle Hardenbergh and 100 sheep to John Neely."

Isabelle jumped when the auctioneer's whip hit her back. She saw her mother and father looking up at her from the crowd.

"Be a good girl, Belle," Ma-Ma Bett cried. "Obey your master." Tears ran down Ma-Ma Bett's cheeks, and she clung to her husband's arm. All of Ma-Ma Bett's children had been taken from her and sold away. Nine-year-old Belle and her little brother, Peter, were the last, and both were being sold today.

Belle wiped the sweat and tears off her face and walked down the wooden steps of the slave block. Her dark, wide eyes were full of sadness, but she straightened her thin shoulders as her new master strode toward her.

He said some words she couldn't understand. He wasn't speaking Dutch, the language Belle had spoken all her life. Her former master, Mr. Hardenbergh, was Dutch (there were many Dutch farmers in New York State), and all of his slaves spoke Dutch. But John Neely did not.

Mr. Neely shouted at Belle and pushed her toward a nervous flock of sheep at the side of the road. Dust swirled as the sheep milled around, keeping away from Neely's barking dogs. Neely shouted again, and the dogs herded the sheep down the road. Belle trotted behind.

The road stretched ahead through forests of oak and maple, across brooks, up and down rolling hills. Belle was covered with dust from her bare toes to her bare head by the time they reached the Neely farm, and she was as thirsty as a dry sponge.

Mr. Neely opened the gate to the sheep pen. The sheep pushed in and dipped their heads into the water tank. "I know how you feel," Belle murmured.

She followed Mr. Neely to the house, brushing the dust off her short dress, her face, arms, and legs. She wanted her mama to be proud of her, if her mama ever heard of her again. But mostly she wanted to be back home. Her bed had been just straw on the muddy ground of the slave cellar, which was always dark and wet, with rats and spiders in the corners, but her mother and father were there.

Belle tipped her head back and stared at the sky. "Oh, Lord," she prayed, "now I'm Belle Neely. Help me be a good girl." The kitchen door banged. A woman stood outside waving a towel at Belle and hollering in a high, screechy voice. Belle's heart sank. Her new mistress didn't sound friendly.

Belle worked for Mrs. Neely for about two years. She learned English as fast as she could so she could understand what the Neelys wanted her to do. Even so her face and back were often sore from slaps and beatings.

One winter day when Belle went out to get firewood, she stopped behind the woodpile. Her bare feet sank into the snow, but she didn't notice the icy cold. She looked up at the leaden sky. "I can't understand it, Lord," Belle said. "Is it right for them to hit me when I work so hard? Ma-Ma Bett said you watch over us. Why don't you help me?"

When spring came Belle's prayer was answered.

The Neelys sold her to Martin Schryver for $105.

The Schryvers' farm was close to the Hudson River and was surrounded by dark woods and granite cliffs. The farm was close to the town school too, but Belle did not go. The Schryvers were kind to Belle, but it probably never occurred to them that she might want to go to school. After all, a slave didn't need book-learning to scrub and clean, wash and iron, and hoe and plant. So Belle never did learn to read or write, but she could speak two languages—English and Dutch.

While Belle was at the Schryvers, she began to make up songs for every occasion. She sang to herself as she walked to town to buy sugar and coffee and calico cloth. She sang as she stood outside the white folks' church and listened to the old hymns. She sang as she fed the chickens and the pigs and wiggled her toes in the soft dirt. She sang as she hoed and weeded the pumpkins and the corn, feeling the warm sun on her long, long legs.

Then in 1810 Mr. Schryver sold her to John Dumont of New Paltz, New York, for a nice profit. That night Mr. Dumont wrote in his account book: "For $300, Belle, about 13 years old, six feet tall."

Dumont soon realized that he had bought a treasure—a tall, strong young woman who could do fieldwork as well as any man and who could also do the inside cleaning and washing. So Belle did both. "She's better to me than a *man*," Dumont told his friends.

Late at night when Belle lay down in the slave kitchen, she always repeated the Lord's Prayer in Dutch, as her mother had taught her. Belle had learned from other slaves that her mother had died and that her father, was being passed from farm to farm, too old to work and almost blind. She desperately wanted to see him again, but Dumont would not let her go. There was too much work to do, he always said.

So of course Belle didn't go. Instead she found a place in the overgrown tangle of willows next to the river where she could tell God how sad she felt.

One day as she hurried to her secret place under the trees, Belle met Bob, a tall young man who belonged to the owner of a neighboring farm. They saw each other often during that summer, and Belle discovered with joy that she could tell Bob what was in her heart. She felt warm with happiness.

But Bob's owner was not happy. If Bob and Belle married, their children would belong to Mr. Dumont. So Bob's owner beat him severely in front of Belle and dragged him away. Belle knew she would never see Bob again.

Soon after that Mr. Dumont had Belle married to one of his own slaves, an old man named Thomas. Belle's first baby, Diana, was born in 1815. When Diana was one month old, Dumont gave Belle permission to visit her father and show him the baby.

Belle wrapped Diana snugly and set out walking toward the farm where her father was last seen. The woods were brilliant with red and orange leaves, and the morning sun softened the frosty bite of the autumn air. Belle began to sing, making up words of joy for the chance to see her father. It had been a long time since she had sung, and her deep, rich voice shook the birds right out of the trees. Belle walked for 12 miles, stopping only a few times to rest and to feed the baby. Then she saw the farm where her father was supposed to be.

Belle held Diana tightly and ran to the slave quarters. But her father was not there. His masters had gotten tired of feeding the old blind man, who had worked for them all his life. They had sent her father with two other elderly slaves to a cabin in the Catskill Mountains, where they were "free" to take care of themselves.

Belle never did see her father again. That winter she learned that all three old people had died in their cabin in the snow.

Belle's baby Diana was growing up healthy and strong, and within a few years, Belle had three more children, a boy she named Peter after her little brother, and two girls, Hannah and Elizabeth. Belle still worked inside, washing and cleaning, and outside in the fields, even though she had four children to tend. She saw that other people, black and white, sometimes did their work poorly and left it that way. But Belle couldn't rest until her work was finished properly. Sometimes she worked all night, leaning against the wall or on her broom to rest.

The other slaves laughed at Belle for working so hard, but Dumont noticed her efforts and praised her. Belle began to think that perhaps Dumont was like God. Her master seemed to see everything she did, and Belle believed that he was as honest as she herself was.

Her son, Peter, was a bright, happy little boy.

Belle often thought how much he was like her younger brother, whom she had not seen since the day they were sold. Belle was thankful that Master Dumont didn't want to sell any of her children, and in fact, according to a new state law, he *could not* sell them outside the state of New York. But when Peter was five years old, Dumont did sell him.

Belle ran to Dumont. "Master," she cried, "you had no right to sell my son!"

"I had every right," Mr. Dumont said. "And it will be good for him. He's going to be a gentleman's servant for Dr. Gedney in New York City."

Belle felt cold inside. She searched frantically for Peter, but he was already gone. She had not even had a chance to say good-bye.

Mr. Dumont was surprised at Belle's reaction. He had always thought that slaves didn't have deep emotions. This belief made it easier for Dumont and other slave owners to buy and sell the children born to slaves. But Belle seemed genuinely upset. So Dumont promised her that if she worked extra hard, he would free her in one year, instead of waiting two years for New York's Freedom Day for all slaves (July 4, 1827).

According to Dumont's promise, Belle would

be free after the next summer's haying time, so she did work extra hard. That winter she often worked most of the night, washing and cleaning, and all day, cooking and mending.

By summertime Belle was so tired that she cut her hand open to the bone while she was harvesting hay. But she couldn't stop. She tied her hand up with the cleanest rag she could find and was soon back at work.

On July 4, 1826, Belle reminded Dumont of his promise and asked for her freedom. He refused. "You didn't work hard enough, Belle," he said. "And you didn't finish the haying when you cut your hand."

Belle stared at him. Dumont was not like God after all. He had made her a promise, but it was just a promise to a slave, not meant to be kept. She could not wait any longer. Belle decided to take her freedom.

Chapter Two

Summer ended. Belle's husband, Thomas, was quite old now, and he expected to live in the Dumonts' slave kitchen for the rest of his life. He didn't care what Belle did. But what was best for her daughters? And where could she go when she left?

Belle pondered these problems while she washed the floors. She thought about them while she smoked the hams and sausages for the winter. She considered what to do while she strung up apples to dry and washed and spun 100 pounds of wool.

Belle finished all the winter preparations so the Dumonts wouldn't be inconvenienced when she left. Then she had a long talk with Diana, Hannah, and Elizabeth. They wanted to stay in the Dumonts' slave kitchen, where they had always lived. Mrs. Dumont liked the girls, and they would be good helpers. Belle knew this was best for them now, but surely after Freedom Day, they would all be together again, including Peter. Belle decided to take only her new baby, Sophie, with her.

One fall morning before dawn, Belle put Sophie on her hip and set off for the farm of a Quaker family who lived just a few miles away. She didn't want to go too far away from her children, and it was known that the Quakers served God and opposed slavery. Belle knew she would find help there.

As the sun spilled over the horizon, Belle knocked on the kitchen door of a tidy stone farmhouse. Before she could say a word, she was invited in. Then Belle stood by the fireplace and explained what she had done.

"We have work for thee here," said Mrs. VanWagener, the Quaker housewife. "Would thou like to stay? We will talk to Mr. Dumont when he comes."

Dumont was there the next day. As Belle had intended, it had not taken him long to find her. She believed he would give her her freedom now. But Dumont wasn't ready to give up a good slave that easily. "You must come back with me!" he thundered.

"No, I won't go," Belle said firmly. "You promised me a year of my time." Mr. VanWagener stepped between them. He offered Mr. Dumont $20 for Belle's services for the year. Dumont took the $20, tipped his hat, and left.

Belle quickly settled into the VanWageners' home, once she had gotten over her surprise at having a whole room just for herself and Sophie. She helped cook and clean and care for the garden, until the VanWageners wondered how they'd gotten along without her. Now she was Belle VanWagener, although the VanWageners said they were not her masters. In fact the VanWageners told her that all people were the same before God.

Belle thought the Quaker home was quiet, very quiet. She never had anything to complain about, so there was no reason to talk to God. She began to feel lonely.

Before long Belle was so lonely that she decided she must return to the Dumonts and her children and slavery. Then one morning she woke up with the feeling that Mr. Dumont would come that day. Mrs. VanWagener shook her head when Belle told her she was going back to Dumont, but she said nothing while Belle folded her extra dress and got Sophie ready.

Later that day Dumont did come. Carrying Sophie, Belle started toward the buggy. But before she reached the gate, something stopped her. "Not another step," a voice said.

For a moment Belle stood still, trembling. Then, clutching Sophie and her bundle of clothes, she turned and ran back into the house. She sat on the edge of her bed and waited for God to strike her dead for trying to go back to slavery, for she knew that it was the voice of the Lord that had stopped her. "Oh, Lord," she cried, "it must be you. I didn't know you were so big."

Belle looked out the window. Dumont was gone. The whole world looked bright and full of glory. She held Sophie tight against her heart and thanked the Lord with a new song of joy. "It was early in the morning," she sang, "just at the break of day...."

At last she dried her eyes, untied her bundle with shaky fingers, and went downstairs where Mrs. VanWagener was waiting. "The Lord did not wish me to return and be a slave," she said.

That fall Belle received terrible news from a passing slave. Five-year-old Peter had been taken to Alabama, the "Deep South." Dr. Gedney had decided that Peter was too small to be his servant and had sold him to his brother Solomon in New

Paltz. And Solomon had sold Peter to a man going to Alabama.

Belle didn't stop to look for Mrs. VanWagener. She bundled up Sophie and raced to Dumont's farm to demand that he get Peter back because he had been sold out of New York State.

Mrs. Dumont answered the door and listened impatiently to Belle's story. "All this fuss over a little nigger," she said with a sniff.

"I will have my child again," Belle insisted. "The Lord will help me. I will have my child again."

The Dumonts would hear no more, so Belle hurried over to Solomon Gedney's farm. But the Gedneys just told Belle to stop making such a disturbance.

Belle walked slowly down the dirt road, away from the farm, not knowing where to go next. She wrapped Sophie tighter in her shawl and tried to sing to her, but there was no music in her heart.

That night she stayed with another Quaker family. The next morning they drove to town in a tall, black buggy and took Belle to the courthouse. Here, the Quaker farmer told her, she would find help to get Peter back. Belle thanked him and climbed down out of the buggy with Sophie.

Her legs felt like shaky willow branches, but she marched straight into the stone courthouse.

Mr. Chip, a lawyer, listened to Belle's story and asked her to swear that the child she wanted really was her son and that he really had been sold South, against the law of the state of New York. Then he wrote out a paper for Belle to give to the constable in New Paltz, where Mr. Gedney lived. Belle thanked Mr. Chip, settled Sophie firmly on her hip, and flew down the courthouse stairs. She walked and ran all the way back to New Paltz, 10 miles down the dusty, rutted road.

When Mr. Gedney saw the lawyer's paper, he realized he'd better get Peter back to New York as fast as he could. He left immediately for Alabama.

Belle returned to the VanWageners and worked and waited all winter for Mr. Gedney to return. Finally, one spring day, she heard that he was back. "The boy is here with me," Gedney said, "but he is mine."

Belle was in a quandary. She didn't want to make Mr. Gedney angry, because he might hurt Peter. But she wanted her son. She *would have* her son. She returned to Mr. Chip, and the lawyer sent another paper to Mr. Gedney.

Mr. Gedney galloped to town and promised angrily to appear in the next session of the court. He left $600 with the court as part of his promise. "Now," Mr. Chip told Belle, "you must wait until next fall when the court meets again. And if Mr. Gedney doesn't show up with Peter, you will get one-half of the $600."

Belle's throat tightened. She tried to explain that she didn't care about the money, it was her son she wanted, and she wanted him back now. Mr. Chip stood up impatiently, said good-bye, and turned back to his papers.

Belle knew the lawyer was getting tired of her. Holding tightly to the rail, she went down the stairs and outside. She stood in the pale spring sunlight and looked back at the stone courthouse. "Oh, Lord," she prayed, "show these people you are my helper." A man passing by, who had seen Belle at the courthouse and knew about her problem, suggested another lawyer who might work more quickly.

Belle gathered her skirts and ran to find the lawyer. The young lawyer told her to bring five dollars and he'd have Peter for her the very next day. Belle's Quaker friends gladly gave her more than five dollars, and she gave it all to the lawyer.

As soon as the sun came up the next morning, Belle knocked on the lawyer's door. "Wait," the lawyer called sleepily from his bedroom window. "Wait until the sun is high. I'll call for you when I'm ready."

That afternoon the lawyer sent for Belle to come to the courthouse. Peter was there with Mr. Gedney. Belle gasped when she saw the bruises on Peter's face and the scars on his thin back. The judge listened to the little boy's owner and to the little boy's mother. When he had heard the whole case, the judge rapped on his desk. "Peter will go with his mother," he said. "Case dismissed."

Belle wanted to sing for joy as she held Peter in her arms. The judge had believed her, a black woman and a former slave, instead of the white man. "Thank you, Lord," she whispered.

A friend from her church offered to take Belle and Peter to New York City where there was a school for black children. But Belle would have to do live-in housework, so there would be no place for her four other children to stay. The older girls again preferred to stay on the Dumonts' farm and wanted Sophie with them too. This was best for now, Belle decided sadly; her dream of having all her family together would have to wait.

Schooling for Peter was more important. So Belle left Sophie with her older sisters and moved to New York City with Peter.

Belle easily found housework in New York and sent Peter, who was now eight, off to school every day through the crowded cobblestone streets. But Peter began to go around with bad boys. Each time he got into trouble, Belle scolded and talked, and Peter would promise to do better. Then he'd get into trouble again.

Peter was in and out of jail during the next 10 years. Belle tried everything she could think of to keep him in school and help him find work. Her heart ached when she saw how the beatings Peter had received in the South had changed him.

Finally Peter found a job as a seaman and sailed from New York harbor on the whaling ship *Zone of Nantucket* in 1839. Belle had high hopes that hard work and fresh sea air would make a new man of her son, and she rejoiced when she received three letters from him asking her not to forget him. She asked friends to read them to her over and over. But then the letters stopped, and Belle never heard from her son again.

Belle was very lonely. She saved every penny she earned, hoping to bring her family to New

York City so they could be together. But the girls and her husband, all freed by New York law in 1827, didn't want to leave the Dumonts' farm.

Belle began to feel that her life was wasted. Her son was gone, and her daughters were content to stay where they had lived in slavery. Her dream of having all her children with her was fading. She asked God what she should do now.

It wasn't long before Belle knew the answer. She was to walk up and down the land, telling others about God's goodness and love for every person.

"The Lord calls me and I must go," she explained to the woman whose wash she did.

"I am no longer the old Belle," she explained to the woman whose mending she did.

Belle gave away all the money she had saved, keeping only twenty-five cents for herself. She put her extra clothes in a pillowcase, tied on her sunbonnet, picked up her walking stick, and left New York City as the sun came up.

She felt like a brand-new person, and as she walked joyfully out of the city, she waited for the Lord to give her a brand-new name. She was no longer Belle Hardenbergh, or Neely, or Dumont, or VanWagener.

The name *Sojourner* came to her mind. A sojourner is a person who goes from place to place, never staying long. The name felt comfortable, like an old friend. "That's it, Lord," she said. "Thank you. And now I need a handle to my name." Belle thought about the last names she'd had from all her different masters. Now the Lord is my master, she thought, and his name is Truth.

"So shall *Truth* be my abiding name until I die," she sang to the clouds drifting overhead. "I am Sojourner Truth."

Chapter Three

It was June 1, 1843, when Sojourner Truth walked out of New York City. She spent part of her twenty-five cents on a boat ride across the East River and then walked east along Long Island's sandy roads. That evening she knocked on a farmhouse door and asked for work in exchange for supper and a place to sleep. The farmer's kind wife wrote a letter for Sojourner to send to her daughters so they wouldn't worry.

Sojourner walked on and in a few days came to a religious camp meeting. There were tents and wagons and people spread out all over the hillside, talking and singing.

Sojourner stopped to do some talking and singing of her own. People gathered around, looking with curiosity at this very tall and very black woman with deep, wise eyes, dressed in a neat Quaker dress and a white shawl, with a white turban on her head. Sojourner told them about her life as a slave. Then in her low voice, as rich and warm as dark maple syrup, she began to sing, "It was early in the morning, just at the break of day...." Her astonished audience listened in awe and asked her to stay a few days so they could hear more.

As the summer passed, Sojourner became well-known at religious meetings in New York and Connecticut and Massachusetts. She talked about what God had done in her life, and she sang songs she'd made up herself. People told others to be sure to go and hear Sojourner Truth.

One evening while Sojourner was at a camp meeting in Massachusetts, a mob of young men appeared. They swarmed through the tents, overturning wagons and swinging bottles and sticks. Sojourner was as frightened as everybody else until she remembered that the Lord would protect her. She decided to help. She got up from her hiding place, smoothed her dress, walked to a small hill, and began to sing. The mob quickly surrounded her, leaving the rest of the camp alone and quiet under the full moon. Sojourner stood calm and unafraid in the midst of the mob, her voice soaring through the treetops, until the young men left the camp meeting in peace.

When all was quiet, Sojourner's friends came out from behind their tents. "You tamed that wild mob," they said, shaking their heads, "with just your voice."

That fall Sojourner traveled to Massachusetts to spend a day in Northampton, a community of people who believed that slavery was wrong and that all people were equal before God. Northampton was not a pretty place. Its large, untidy factory buildings were surrounded by bare, frozen meadows. Men, women, and children worked side by side raising silkworms and making silk cloth. No one had time to cook properly or clean or do the laundry. Sojourner could do all these things, so she decided to stay and help for a while. As she worked, she had the children read passages to her from the Bible so she could memorize them.

It was in Northampton that, for the first time, Sojourner was introduced to people who were determined to stop slavery. She met people who were traveling all over New York and many other northern states to explain how and why slavery must end. She met William Lloyd Garrison and other abolitionists, people who were devoting their lives to the fight against slavery. And she met

Frederick Douglass, a fiery young black man who had escaped from slavery in 1838. Sojourner listened eagerly to the talk about the antislavery meetings these men were holding, and she added their ideas to her own knowledge of slavery.

In 1849 Sojourner went back to New Paltz to visit her daughters. Only Diana was there. The other girls were married and gone. Sojourner grieved over the lost years spent in New York City, over Peter's disappearance, and over her daughters growing up without her. She promised herself once again that someday she would have her own house and her children around her.

When Sojourner returned to Northampton, she found that the arguments over slavery were getting hotter. Congress passed a new and harsher fugitive slave law, which said that anyone who helped a slave escape could be put in prison. Although slavery was now prohibited in the northern states, a freed slave in the North could be dragged South if two white men swore that he or she was escaped property. Many northerners thought this was outrageous. More people began to listen to the antislavery speakers.

The story of Frederick Douglass's life as a southern slave was published in 1845. But the story of a southern slave did not convince people in the North that slavery had to be stopped. Abolitionists thought the story of a *northern* slave—Sojourner Truth, for example—might do the job.

So Sojourner told the story of her life to a friend. In 1850 *The Narrative of Sojourner Truth: A Northern Slave* was published—a thin, brown paper-covered book with Sojourner's picture on the first page.

Sojourner filled her carpetbag with copies of her book and set off for antislavery meetings throughout the northern United States. At first she only listened to the other speakers, but one evening Mr. Garrison told the audience that Sojourner Truth would be the first speaker.

Sojourner knew that the next speaker would be Wendell Phillips, a well-known abolitionist, and she wondered what she could say to be different from him. What could she do to make people remember what she said? She decided to sing a new song she had made up about black men and women in slavery.

Sojourner walked confidently to the speakers' platform, dressed as always in plain Quaker style. In her strong, deep voice she began to sing, "I am pleading for my people, a poor down-trodden race, who dwell in freedom's boasted land with no abiding place...."

After the meeting people crowded around Sojourner asking for copies of her "homemade" songs and for her book and for pictures (Sojourner called them "shadows") of herself.

She soon became one of the most powerful speakers in the antislavery fight and one of the few black women to speak to white audiences.

Sojourner met many women—Amy Post, Lucretia Mott, and others—who raised money for the abolitionists, taught former slaves to read and write, and helped slaves escape on the Underground Railroad. (The Underground Railroad was not a railroad that ran underground. It was a network of safe houses where escaped slaves could hide on the long, dangerous journey to Canada, where they would be free.) From these women Sojourner learned about another fight. This one was for women's rights. In 1850 a woman could not vote or own property. Many of the men who opposed slavery, including Frederick Douglass, also spoke out for women's rights. After all, they agreed, when we see one injustice we see the other as well. Sojourner, being a woman, gladly joined the fight for women's rights too.

Some women did not welcome her. They feared that if women's rights got mixed up with the antislavery fight, both would fail. Sojourner soon proved them wrong.

In 1851 she attended the Women's Rights Convention in Akron, Ohio. As the meeting progressed, men in the audience began to ridicule the women for wanting to be treated as men's equals. "Women are weak," they shouted. "Weak in body and weak in mind. Women have to be taken care of by men."

Sojourner looked around. No one seemed to know what to do. She set her sunbonnet down and slowly stood up. "Don't let her speak," some of the women said loudly.

But chairwoman Frances Gage, who was trying to quiet the audience, smiled with relief. "Sojourner Truth," she announced.

Sojourner looked quietly at the scoffing crowd. Then she pointed to the man who had just spoken. "That man over there," she said in her powerful voice, "that man says that women need to be helped into carriages and lifted over ditches and have the best place everywhere. Nobody ever helps me into carriages or over mud puddles or gives me any best place! And ain't I a woman?"

Sojourner pushed up one sleeve. "Look at my arm! I have plowed and planted and gathered into barns, and no man could beat me! And ain't I a woman? I could work as much and eat as much as a man—when I could get it—and bear the lash as well! And ain't I a woman?"

Then Sojourner raised her arms toward heaven. "I have borne five children and seen most all sold off into slavery, and when I cried out with a mother's grief, none but Jesus heard! And ain't I a woman?"

The crowd sat in stunned silence, hardly daring to breathe. Sojourner finished and sat down on the steps again. Then the audience, women and men, wiped their eyes and applauded wildly. "You reached our hearts," one man called.

Mrs. Gage wrote later, "She picked us up in her strong arms and carried us over the difficulties. She turned the tide in our favor. I have never in my life seen anything like her magical influence."

For two years Sojourner traveled throughout Ohio with a borrowed horse and buggy and 600 copies of her *Narrative*. She held her own meetings, and she spoke at every abolitionist and women's rights meeting within horse-trotting distance. She bounced over rutted roads and past hills covered with dark forests; she drove by log cabins and sturdy farmhouses. When she came to a town, she'd stop her horse in the middle of the street and begin to sing. That got people's attention. Then Sojourner would speak, and that kept people's attention.

One day after she had finished, a man said to her, "Old woman, I don't care any more for your talk than I do for the bite of a flea."

Sojourner's eyes sparkled. "Perhaps not," she said, "but Lord willing, I'll keep you scratching."

Another time Sojourner was on the speakers' platform with several other abolitionists when a violent rainstorm began. As the thunder crashed outside, a small man jumped up from the audience. "I'm afraid to be in the same room with you," he cried. There was a second roll of thunder and the building shook. "You see," he went on, "this is the wrath of God coming down on me for listening to you say that slaves should be free and women should be equal with men."

Sojourner rose majestically in her plain, dark green dress. "Now, child," she said comfortingly, "don't be scared. I don't expect God's ever *heard* of you." The audience roared with laughter as she sat down.

Even though more and more people listened to the abolitionists, slavery seemed to be winning. In 1854 Congress passed the Kansas-Nebraska Act, which said settlers could decide the slavery question for themselves. In 1857 the Supreme Court ruled that Dred Scott, a black slave, had no rights in the United States, nor did any slave. Slaves were just property, the Court said.

One evening Sojourner was in the front row at Faneuil Hall in Boston when Frederick Douglass spoke. Douglass was discouraged and said that the struggle to stop slavery would end in blood. No one moved. Then Sojourner stood and pointed her long finger at Douglass. "Frederick," she roared, "Frederick, is God dead?" But Sojourner was discouraged too, for her people were still in slavery in the South, and there was no sign that it would end.

The fight to end slavery spread west: to Ohio, with its web of underground railroads; to Michigan, where fleeing slaves tried to escape to Canada; to Kansas, where settlers were fighting to decide whether they would allow slavery in their territory.

Sojourner went alone to Ohio, Illinois, Indiana, and Michigan, to sing and speak against slavery and in support of women's rights. Her friends worried that she would be hurt or killed by mobs, but Sojourner said, "The Lord will preserve me . . . for the truth is powerful and will prevail."

Angry mobs often tried to break up abolitionist meetings with clubs or stones, and in one town a group of furious men surrounded Sojourner's buggy shouting that they would burn down the building if she tried to speak. Sojourner looked at them calmly through her steel-rimmed spectacles. "Then I'll speak on the ashes," she said and drove on.

In 1860 Abraham Lincoln was elected president. "If slavery is not wrong," Lincoln said, "then nothing is wrong." At last, said the abolitionists, an end to slavery.

But in April 1861, just a few weeks after Lincoln took office, the southern states left the Union to set up a country of their own in which they could have all the slaves they wanted. The new president refused to let the United States be divided. The Civil War began.

After all Sojourner's speaking and singing, there was still no end to slavery.

Chapter Four

Sojourner was deeply discouraged. She needed to rest for a while. With money from her book, she bought a little wooden house in Battle Creek, Michigan. Sojourner put her favorite pictures on the walls and filled the house with flowers. Her daughters and two grandsons, Sammy Banks and James Caldwell, came to live with her. (Her husband, Thomas, had died.) At last, as she had promised herself long ago, Sojourner had her family together.

Then, on January 1, 1863, 20 years after Sojourner had started preaching and singing against slavery, President Lincoln signed the Emancipation Proclamation. This was what Sojourner had worked and prayed for. Her people were free. She rejoiced and praised God and sang her favorite song, "It was early in the morning, just at the break of day...." Then she wondered if the Lord had any more work for her.

Every evening, as Sojourner sat on the front porch with her family, Sammy read aloud from the newspaper. The news was bad. The war dragged on and soldiers were dying. Sojourner's heart ached. She decided to go to Washington, D.C., to see President Lincoln for herself. She would take 11-year-old Sammy with her. Her grandson James had already left, dressed in his 54th Massachusetts Regiment uniform. He had gone to fight for the Union.

Sojourner and Sammy left Battle Creek in 1864, in June when the roads were dry. They traveled by foot, buggy, and train. Sojourner was asked to speak in almost every town they passed through. She was more famous than ever now because Harriet Beecher Stowe (the author of a famous book about slavery called *Uncle Tom's Cabin*) had written a long article about her, which had appeared in the *Atlantic Monthly*. "I do not recollect ever to have [met] any one who had more...silent and subtle power...than this woman," Mrs. Stowe wrote. Mrs. Stowe compared Sojourner to a princess and said that she stood at ease in a roomful of ministers, as calm and erect as a desert palm tree.

It was September before Sojourner and her

grandson arrived in Washington. In October she met President Lincoln. He greeted her warmly and said he had heard about her many times.

"You are the best president we have had," Sojourner said.

"Thank you," Lincoln replied, "but those before me would have done just as I have done if the time had come."

Sojourner and Sammy had stayed with friends while waiting to see President Lincoln. Sojourner's friends took her around the city. She saw thousands of former slaves who had walked to "Mr. Lincoln's city" and were living in shacks and tents and mud and filth.

Sojourner was horrified. She went straight to the freedman's bureau, an agency run by the army to care for former slaves, to offer her help. They sent her to Freedman's Village, just outside Washington, where there was housing for some of the former slaves. Sojourner pushed up her sleeves, tied on an apron, and went right to work.

"Be clean! Be clean!" she reminded the women daily. She taught the former field-workers how to cook and how to mend and wash their clothes, and she made sure the children went to the Freedman's Village school.

Sojourner sent a letter to her family and friends (Sammy wrote it). "I judge it is the will of both God and the people that I should remain in Washington," she said.

At last, in April 1865, the Civil War was over. The United States was united again. One week later President Lincoln was dead—shot by a man who thought the South should have won the war. Sojourner walked through the streets of Washington with a heavy heart. She tried to sing, but could only whisper, "I am pleading for my people...."

In September the War Department asked Sojourner to work as a nurse at the Freedman's Hospital in Washington. She began immediately, encouraging patients, instructing and helping nurses, and trying to find supplies for the hospital.

One afternoon as Sojourner walked back to the hospital with an armful of blankets, she was so tired she just couldn't walk any more. Horse-drawn streetcars clanged up and down the road, filled with white folks. Sojourner waited for a car to stop, but none did. Finally, as yet another car passed her, she called out, "I want to ride!" People crowded around, the horses stopped, and Sojourner got on. The conductor was furious and demanded she get off. Sojourner settled back in her seat.

"I'm not someone from the South," she said firmly. "I'm from the Empire State of New York, and I know the law as well as you do."

The next day she tried to ride another streetcar. Again the conductor would not stop. Sojourner ran after the car and caught up with it. When the horses stopped, she jumped on. "What a shame," she panted, "to make a lady run so." The conductor threatened to throw her off. "If you try," she said, "it will cost you more than your car and horses are worth." He didn't.

The third time Sojourner tried to ride a streetcar, she was with a white friend. "Stand back, nigger," shouted the conductor to Sojourner, "and let that lady on."

"*I* am a lady too," said Sojourner, and she stepped aboard with her friend.

A few weeks later, after more experiences with Sojourner Truth, the president of the streetcar company told his conductors that they were to stop for everybody, or they would be fired. The next day Sojourner smiled when she looked at the street cars. "Look," she said to a friend, "the insides of the cars look like pepper and salt."

But as Sojourner rode through the streets, she saw the former slaves living in hovels on swampy land, crowded together without fresh air or sunlight. There was no more room in Freedman's Village; there was no work in Washington for people who only knew farming; and there was no hope for the children, who had no future at all.

The new president and the Congress did not see the need to help the former slaves. After all, the slaves had been freed. Now they could take care of themselves.

Sojourner knew she had one more job to do.

Chapter Five

In 1870, when she was about 73 years old, Sojourner explained her plan to President Grant and Congress. "You're giving away land in the West to rich railroad companies." She leaned forward on her cane. "Give some western land to these freedmen. They helped build this country with their blood and sweat, and they have nothing." Sojourner's voice was as powerful as ever, and there was anger in it. "Give them land, give them tools to work with so they can settle this land and be a people."

The congressmen applauded her speech and shook her hand. Then they said that nothing could be done unless the people of the United States demanded it. ("The people" meant white men, as women and blacks could not vote.)

Sojourner and Sammy set out to talk to the people of the United States, so they would know what to demand. And Sojourner took stacks of petitions for them to sign, so she could show Congress what the people wanted.

In meeting after meeting, state after state, Sojourner described how the former slaves were living in Washington. "Help them, teach them to work for themselves," she explained over and over. "You owe it to them. You took away from them all they earned and made them what they are."

Thousands of people came to hear Sojourner and sign her petition. But nothing changed in Washington. "Give them land and something to start with, and have teachers teach them how to read," she repeated. "Then they can be somebody."

One night in Providence, Rhode Island, Sojourner lost her patience with white men. "With all your opportunities for reading and writing," she roared, thumping her cane on the floor, "you don't take hold and do anything. I wonder what you are in the world for!"

Sojourner and Sammy traveled through Rhode Island, Massachusetts, New York, Michigan, Kansas, Iowa, Illinois, Missouri, Wisconsin, Ohio, and New Jersey. In the summer of 1874, they returned to Washington carrying rolls of petitions.

But Congress refused to act.

Sojourner did not continue the fight. Sammy was very sick, so sick that Sojourner immediately took him home to Battle Creek, away from the dusty heat of Washington. In February he died. Sojourner's heart was broken. She put the neatly tied petitions on a shelf and didn't look at them again.

In 1877 Sojourner heard that the former slaves were doing for themselves what she had been asking for all along. They were moving West. By 1879 thousands of former slaves had moved to Kansas to begin new lives.

In late 1879, when she was about 83 years old, Sojourner traveled to Kansas to see for herself the fruits of her labor. She saw her people working on their own land, learning to read and write, becoming somebody. "Thank you, Lord," she whispered. "You've given me a new song."

The Travels of Sojourner Truth

Sojourner Truth devoted much of the second half of her life to speaking out against slavery and campaigning for women's rights. Her travels took her to more than 20 states throughout New England and the Midwest. Sojourner was born into slavery in Ulster County, New York (1). After she was freed in 1827, she lived in various cities, including New York, New York (2); Northampton, Massachusetts (3); Battle Creek, Michigan (4); and Washington, D.C. (5).

AFTERWORD

Her trip to Kansas was Sojourner's last journey. She returned to Battle Creek, where she worked and lived until her death in 1883. Her children and grandchildren were with her when she died.

"Don't fret, child," she said to one of the

children at her bedside, "I'm going home like a shooting star."

She was buried in her plain, dark dress, with a white scarf around her neck and a white turban over her gray hair—a beloved woman whose voice had helped free her people.

MORE ABOUT SOJOURNER TRUTH

1. There is some variation in the spelling of names from Sojourner Truth's early history. Some sources refer to the young Sojourner as *Isabella* instead of *Isabelle*. *Neely* is often spelled *Nealy*, and *Schryver* can be found as *Scriver* or *Schriver*.

2. It is believed that the ship *Nantucket* went down in a storm at sea, with Sojourner's son, Peter, on board.

3. The "Ain't I a Woman" speech in the 1850 edition of Sojourner Truth's *Narrative* said, "I have borne 13 children..." This was corrected in the 1884 edition to read, "I have borne 5 children..."

4. The Emancipation Proclamation said that after January 1, 1863, "all persons held as slaves within any States...in rebellion against the United States shall be...forever free." The southern slaves were actually freed only when the Union army advanced into the southern states. The 13th Amendment, passed in 1865, officially abolished slavery in the United States.